Uncensored Snapshots

Cover image by Abdulsalam Abdul [Instagram: art_lithiumf]
Author's photo by FatherCat
Edited by Maria S. Picone
Cover design by James Rawlings, and Teresa Snow

Chestnut Review Chapbooks, an imprint of Chestnut Review LLC
Ithaca, New York

https://chestnutreview.com
ISBN: 978-1-965158-16-6

Uncensored Snapshots

Zaynab Iliyasu Bobi

Chestnut Review Chapbooks

CONTENTS

Praise for Zaynab Ilyasu Bobi's
Uncensored Shapshots

The poems in this collection hold a mirror up to massacre. The strength of *Uncensored Snapshots* lies not only in its ability to capture the reader but to haunt them. As each page details a new horror, we are left wondering: how much taller can cruelty become? Where do you go when everywhere kills you? This chapbook is grief in capital letters, a message to a country that runs away and toward fire. And yet, Zaynab's language is so brightly alive. Her attention to rhythm, image, and storytelling speaks to her poetic genius, creating an entry point into the speaker's tilted sanity. You will walk away from this book transformed. Long after reading I still feel its echo: "to hear the screeching sound of my mother's cry. i heard it & i hated it. ya Allah, i heard it & i hated it."

— Nicole Adabunu, MFA Poetry Graduate, Iowa Writers' Workshop '23 and Cave Canem Fellow '24

In *Uncensored Snapshots*, Nigerian-Hausa poet Zaynab Iliyasu Bobi explores identity, displacement, and resilience with unflinching precision. Drawing from her background in medical laboratory science and digital artistry, she creates a multifaceted lens through which to examine loss and transformation. Particularly through the lens of Boko Haram's impact, Zaynab creates tangible manifestations of fragmentation that mirror exile and dislocation. Zaynab navigates different kinds of loss with profound sensitivity, charting both grief and the greater political dimensions of conflict. Uncensored Snapshots bears witness to the search for humanity in a world marked by erasure; through Zaynab's fearless exploration of poetic form, personal fragments metamorphose into a collective cry to be heard.

— Cara Waterfall, award-winning poet & author, *Radiant Wound* (Unsolicited Press, May 2025)

In *Uncensored Snapshots*, we witness firsthand poignant reflections by audacious speakers on personal and societal struggles saddling many communities stuck in a nexus of tragic events. Zaynab's brilliance shines through the myriad fashion with which these poems concurrently serve as a reminder of the similarity of our realities as a people and a plea for the rehumanization of our existence.

— Abu Bakr Sadiq, author of *Leaked Footages*

road to freedom?

every news from the phone
    drains our blood to the nails.

after three rings, you will know death
    lurks in the air.

i don't think the media can tell the road to Mariga,
    Birnin Gwari, Ukuru, & a lot more.

 i fear if i name them all,
    they will vanish.

here is the reality: the dead are buried, & the survivors
    are forced to forget.

just because a body knows blood doesn't mean
    it should swim in its stain.

there are many ways to freedom
    without loving the knife.

i think these days, surviving can pass
    for an obligation.

all my people wanted was to exist
    outside something less suffocating

like the question mark that continued to drag the bluebirds
    out of their bodies.

like the hands that hauled the drowned from the large mouth
    of the Atlantic.

the ritual

it began like a warning

then a ritual. the phone would ring,

& my parents would answer.

innalillahi wa inna illaihi raji'un.

Allah ya jikan su. Allah ya bayyanar dasu.

these became a mantra my parents

shared with the person at the other end.

how the news catches us

off guard even when we know

where it sleeps surprises me.

this time was different.

just like the others before it.

i had just returned home from school.

& the first thing my mother said

was *Alhamdulillah muta tayi araha—*

our way of saying gratitude

for not being swallowed by the road

after the kisses, the phone rang. my parents

looked at each other & started to rehearse the mantra—

which one will it be: dead or kidnapped?

toxic laughing gas

at the verification center
a lecturer scanned my face

& inquired about my people.
i looked at him, & we both

burst our laughter into the air.
every one came out like a crow

but that didn't stop us
from gathering. the thing is,

deep down, we could feel tiny
blackbirds eating out of it.

but we continued laughing
until there was nowhere else

for them to go. for us to go.
at the end, we swallowed & passed

the graveyard before our eyes.

martyr of daily bread

Ra'afat Al-issa was killed by Israeli soldiers as he traveled
through a breach in the apartheid wall on his way to work.
He is now known as the "martyr of daily bread."

By Mariam Barghouti on Mondoweiss. 10th November, 2022.

Ra'afat   رافت   means pity in Arabic.   means
compassion.   means kindness.

translates to water's softened   hands. translates to the wind's un-
ruined   teeth.   10th November, 2022   Ra'afat›s name was
stripped of   meaning.   Ra'afat's body

was mapped with bullets.   Ra'afat became the antonym   of his
name   in a blood bag.

he became the seeker of his name: pity, kindness. Ra'afat was named
martyr of daily bread.

i know now how names are given   how the blood trails to where the
feet last touched.

say   the soldiers   asked his name   before they made a country
of bullets in his body

and   he said   انا رافت,   انا رافت   i am compassion,
i am kindness.

say they asked him   about the water,   if it did not ripple
when pebbles were thrown.

he would have said   انا فقط عابر سبيل ,انا فقط عابر سبيل,   i am
only a passerby, i am only a passerby.

say   Ra'afat had a bar mitzvah at 13,   would he house   a bullet in
this head?   would his face

hold a scar that says, shoot me, shoot me,   make of my home   a war
field? would kindness be a body bag?

martyr

انا رافت

i am only a passerby,   i am only a passerby.

انا رافت

i am only a passerby,   i am only a passerby.

the calling

how a man runs   until he catches the wind   baffles us.

it's as if the time   slows down to take a rest   & forget

to tick.   this happens a lot where we come from

& in all the places, wealth,   as gravity,   takes a hold.

the only force in play is   power. dreams have no place.

they say anything that rusts,   breathes & answers the call of water.

we wonder how an ocean   passes through   a body, broken,

full of metal without spilling, rusting.   some say it's a miracle,

we say it is *debt*.   because here,   there is no miracle

without a claim. at the cliff,   one-third   of every night passes

& a sound follows—creates waves that resonate   into prayers.

but   we shattered beings   always distort the wave

to make   a disturbance   that reverberates into pain.

yes, we are broken   but would you blame us— they teach us

to stay out of the light   & watch our shadows   disappear.

how to knot a hausa tongue

standing on the fodium,

frefaring to give a speech

on how to pasten a tongue,

i make my **c** hold its reflection

on every p-word

that four out of my moutz

to stof me prom fronounzing

words like fretty, feefle, fray, fain

wrongly and at the tif where my tongue

is a measure of how much English

it can hold without breaking,

slightly tight to porm a bridge

between my voice and the mic,

i end the sfeech saying,

flease, learn to ferfect your fronounzations.

sank you.

origin of the guns

most times, i deprive my poems of names
because in my language, safety loses itself to fear.

i might find my head cut off when the government reads this.
why does the truth share so many enemies when it's already bitter?

before writing this poem, i rewatched the interrogation video
of a captured bandit, face blurred, about the origin of the guns.

the media might have turned off their cameras but know this:
in Dinya, there is a white helicopter airdropping guns at the heart

of a forest the government is *still learning the coordinates to*.
i call this bullshit, lies, but who am i to say that out loud

& still have my tongue rolling in my mouth. it wasn't night
as you would all imagine—since evil shares a gene with darkness.

it was during the day, bright & awake. i'm not calling names,
but how can a country's airspace host a rusty helicopter with no invite.

i do want to believe that all hands are unstained, but i›m out of options.
my people are dying. my people are dying. i need to believe in something.

everyone tends to care when you pass through the blade

for Aunty H

the place i come from, there are words that make it

out of darkness after the eyes close their doors.

da mun sani—the last time i heard them,

aunty H gathered her husband's punches in her heart.

at the hospital, the doctor drew the white sheet

and said it was heart failure. we knew

it was the aster meals her mother fed her on every visit.

God knows we added more to the ingredients.

when she came home with patches like an abandoned

sidewalk, her eyes threatening to spill a river,

we gave her a handkerchief & passed a bowl of freshly

made aster meal. because that is what we, women, do.

i swear, we walked into her broken bones,

built a fort of excuses & kept going.

is this what you call love? do you not see where the seeds

of your selfish love sprouted—into her grave?

mother, hear me, when your daughter comes home,

add softness to her meal. the living also deserve roses.

helium

it is a dark day. there are birds singing.
i would have made roses out of the songs

if i knew their names. i'm bad at naming.
once, i got a yellow bear face doll,

& named her Slippery. she kept slipping
out of my hands when i first held her.

i wonder if that is why my body can't contain
the sun even in the cold hours of the evening.

i know we are both burning, but this body needs to fly.
you see, with the sun in my mouth, the helium will lift

me up. we will both fly away from this misery. i & my body.
i don't mind if i burst. it is my new language of happiness.

isn't that what happens when people
begin to laugh?

Baƙin ciki

the most lively room in the house is my mother's. there is al-
ways something playing on the tv when you get in. a qira'a from
a sheik or tafsir to dadin kowa on arewa24. this time, a cloud
settled in every corner. when i entered to greet her, the only light
that allowed my feet to take a second step was the light rays that
slipped in when i opened the door. the disco lights were turned
off. every joy was dosed to sleep by the grief lurking in the
room. you would always find her on her dadduma with a tasbih
in her hand. this time it was different. i could hear tiny sobs
sinking out of her mouth. slowly, i closed the door and went
back. believe me, i wanted to know how she slept, but i didn't
know how i would control myself when i said *ina kwana* and she
asked *if it was morning yet?*

a broken constellation

Many villagers are feared dead following a bomb allegedly dropped by a Nigerian Air Force jet during a Maulud celebration at Tudun Biri, a community within Igabi Local Government Area of Kaduna State.
4th December, Daily Trust.

at
the begin
-ning, the constellation
was of villagers plaiting graceful
cornrows on earth's scanty hair. they were
all alive, the stars, souls, before the bomb-rain, be
-fore the river held in it the resemblance of veins, in Tudun
Biri. the babies still sipped stars from their mother's breast, the people
hadn't smelled the burning flesh of their loved ones, & they had yet to pick
the remains of their deaths from the trees. clocking to the present, i was never
meant to write this poem. i was supposed to teach my keyboard the mechanism
of silence, or make an emoji of how another military *mistake* marred a mill
-ion faces. but how do i tell my *country's pride* that a few miles from
the village are lungs suffocating in the toxic air of banditry?
after the first bomb blast, there were only a few stars
left in the sky & the constellation had no me
-mory of another throw thirty minutes
later. the ~~survivor's~~ helpers' blood
hadn't spilled & the sky
was only half
blind with
smoke.

oh my country, do you still have more to offer,
or are the casualties enough for today?
what i want to know is, can we pray Janazah
or dig more graves for the survivors, for us?

the event

i've been trying to teach myself how to unthread
my memories of that day—the first time the phone

call about my grandfather's kidnapping came in, a bag
of soot. with the way silence sealed the room,

i'd never have thought it was the air's way of gathering
enough waves to flood our eyes with a river of grief.

assalamu alaikum—the peace that managed to hold
our sorrows at bay after answering the calls.

it happened so fast—the phone call to the afterward event.
they say there is a first for everything, but Allah knows,

i wish this first erased itself before it existed.
in my wildest dreams, i have never wished for my ears

to hear the screeching sound of my mother's cry.
i heard it & i hated it. ya Allah, i heard it & i hated it.

bless the broken

every phone call resets our sorrow to default.
when the news pours out of the transmission waves,

our minds become porous:
will we ever see our loved ones alive?

people said my uncle's body sought asylum
in the stars when the bullets were launched.

i guessed his cheekbones were too proud; they begged for a spot
in the night's breast. i haven't seen him since

but my aunty said, *in the morning, in front of the mirror, he
searches every corner of his face, looking for an un-ruined*

version of himself—a man without nightmares hidden
in his scars. i fear what solitude does to a man, how it strips

his sanity, paving way for madness to sneak in. but how faint
can a shadow become?

he is alive. that is the most important thing.
Allah knows my people crawl out of darkness when rescued.

i have seen their laughter drill black holes in the walls.
no wonder people go mute after returning home. as if

all they could muster was blinking. we trace every tear
to the ground to see how far it would spread.

can you imagine what they would say
when they breathe in freedom?

the river

for women widowed by Boko Haram

no one leaves home unless home is the mouth of a shark.

Warsan Shire.

i will tell you about the mother   of three
& the children she hasn't lost   yet.
keep the count   because what is lost remains lost.
remember   she hasn't lost them yet.
one of the son's mouths   hasn't been purged
to cough out blood.   & the river   is far away
from where i stand   to write this poem.
let's do a bit of retelling.   i will start
from the beginning.   i promise   no one
will be lost.   what is lost   remains lost.
the river.   no one knows the aches   of the mother
like the river.   but before the river,   there was a home.
God,   i hate quietness, said   the loud cries from guns.
i know you will be wondering   about the husband.
don't worry about the puffy eyes   of her sons.
instead, you would find her head-tie   on her husband's face.
there was a downfall   & the sons   witnessed it, too.
that is all i can tell you.   what is lost remains lost.

imagine you are standing   by the riverbed

& the mother   is there, too.   & another woman is

breastfeeding a child   she would later throw   into the river.

don't call it cruelty. a mother knows all about love

& its burden. what is lost   remains lost.

how to bargain for a loved one's ransom

i did not pluck the chicken feathers.

i close the kitchen door & open a portal

into this poem. i know you are wondering

why i start from the end.

that is where the body rests—cold & bloody.

if this kind of death can be called *rest*.

it has been many years since i was frightened.

i've heard a lot about catastrophes. i have seen them too.

there is nothing about loss that i haven›t felt.

tonight, i will practice how to answer

the phone calls. how to cut my rage

into tiny pieces of gentleness—

ranku shi dade, Allah ya huce zuciyar ku, dan labai—

because last time, my uncle lost a limb

& children died in captivity. at this moment,

roaring thoughts haul my mind.

scream until you lose the voices.

with my ice-cold fingers, i held the phone to my ears,

dan labai, nawa zamu biya wannan karar?

i need to know how much my son's head will cost.

caged

there are times when the phone rings

    & i want to decline wishing

the bad news will lose its relativity

    & bounce out of time.

people often ask *why don't you speak up?*

    why not take your voice to the street?

why not pick a white flag

    that might end up dyed in your blood?

God knows i have always wanted

    to scream & say *i swear we are not cowards.*

they would be waiting for us there—all of them.

    like they caught up with the people before us.

what is worse than seeing your freedom

    imprison itself just to keep you safe.

escaping the home i called body

sometimes, all i want is to travel past my skin
into my veins, drill the hardness off my bones

& swim in its marrow—just to tell myself
that i have been enough even before my mind

reshaped my fears into beings. at both ends of my journey,
i'm burning. i repeat what i always say to the fire:

not today. i will not let you arrange yourself into a rife of grief
just to see how beautifully pain would sit on my face.

everything with an opening deserves to let it out.
last night, after many years, i opened my mouth

& all the words mumped the bluebirds hauling in the sky
to the coroner. & i knew the marrows, too, had hues

of brokenness in them. see how my mouth holds songs
too dark for the night? i can't tie this on anatomy—

says bone marrow declines with age. i know best

than to chide the changes in my body on aging—

evidence of how time dragged life out of us. believe me,

old age is still running miles behind. it is no surprise

i'm a heap of broken things. i love the endings of poems

because that is where i break open myself,

lay every piece in the lines & let them form strings of birds.

she was, she was

i know that i keep mentioning my uncle.
yes, my uncle. he was. until he was not.

just like the people kidnapped that day
and the other days before that.

i fear visiting my village. we all fear going back.
it is a long journey, we say. but the truth is,
we are scared of trading our present for past tense.

i'm scared of waking up
the next morning with a bullet in my chest,
hearing people saying:

who should we blame for the rotten fruits?

after The Nigerian Nightmare by Chinedu Gospel

i was never meant to say anything.

i was supposed to watch the fruits

grow in the garden of snakes.

yesterday, i took a cyborg to my country

for sightseeing & told him to zip

his mouth about the rotten.

his cheeks still hold a warning tag

from the last visit. at the lab,

i told the prosthetic to cover

the cyborg's cheeks with my country's

coat of arms—the eagle on the top

& the horses posing on both sides.

i understand little about dishonesty

but surviving a political nightmare

is to take from the rotten

or embrace the holiness of silence.

the cyborg & i—since we arrived—

have been fasting from our blue-coated tongue.

when the cyborg departed for home,

i formatted his memory

because the ears between ruins & truth

are deaf & i do not want another cyborg's chip to rust.

i swear, i do not want to blame my countrymen,

but who hasn't eaten from the garden?

finding my way home.

yes, i sang with a bluebird last night. yes, my tongue was folded.
yes, my door was locked. yes, i didn't hold the knife. yes, the
knife held me. yes, i threw time out the window. yes, the win-
dow was the size of a grave. yes, i ran with the wind. yes, i
touched the sky. yes, i fell on the ground. yes, it was a maze.
yes, i was home. yes, i was still on the road. yes, a road can be a
home. yes, it depends on how long you have walked.

Invisibility

Law of invisibility: arrange the atoms in a solid object randomly. Heat at high temperature and cool down immediately.

There is a realm in my mouth.

In my mouth, there is a dream

In the dream, men are wingless canaries

And water is extinct from the breast of the sea.

With the day scattered over the body I can't keep,

I filtered the sun and sang the moon into the ears of the night.

Isn't this what the body does—asking for what it can't have?

I fought for my breath to remain in my lungs,

But I lost it when I chanted *a bamu tsaro*, give us security.

As if to say, my mouth whiffed out *a bamu tsoro*, give us fear.

I hoisted a white flag on the street, and my mother buried another child.

I have seen home scraped out of the anatomy of its name,

Children blown until they are as weightless as their dreams

And their mothers' bodies evolved into chrysanthemums.

I wonder if this country is another form of exile.

Chased from home,

Heated under the sun's gathering skirt

And drowned in other names of water—

ghazal with home

the trace left of my origin is my memory, dug from the fossil of مسكان

the men hauled into the ebbing tides of the sea—with no map of مسكان

it felt like yesterday, music blaring from the neighborhood radio, مسكان

and women and children all danced to Choge's newest hit of مسكان

the men first came in shadows and we gave them نور

watered their hands without knowing it would choke the airways of مسكان

just before we boarded the boat, i saw her, my mother, burning our identities

then made me open my mouth for the wind to blow the remains of مسكان

i played dumb for three days when we arrived on the other side

because whenever spoken to, mama covered my mouth and said, no trace of مسكان

at the park, when i saw a man praying—head kissing the loamy rug of earth—

i sniffed the fragrance hidden in my name, زينب —is this not the smell of مسكان ?

Acknowledgements

I would like to extend my gratitude to the editors of the magazines, journals, and anthologies in which the earlier versions of these poems first appeared.

Arc Poetry Magazine: Martyr of Daily Bread

Cutbank: Finding My Way Home

Torch Literary Arts: A Speech on How to Knot A Hausa Tongue

Poetry Wales: the calling

The Deadland: the river

PoetryColumn: Invisibility

Who should we blame for the rotten fruits? Won the 2023 Labari Prize in Poetry.

About the Author

Zaynab Iliyasu Bobi, Frontier I, is a Nigerian-Hausa poet, multidisciplinary artist, and a Medical Laboratory Scientist from Bobi. She is the author of *Cadaver of Red Roses* (O, Miami Books) won the 2024 Derricotte/Eady Chapbook Prize, winner of the inaugural Folorunsho Editor's Poetry Prize 2023, Labari Poetry Prize 2023, the inaugural Akachi Chukwuemeka Prize for Literature 2023, Gimba Suleiman Hassan Gimba ESQ Poetry Prize, 2022, and was named honorable mention for the 2025 Elizabeth Alexander Creative Writing Award (EACWA) for poetry. Zaynab is the first beneficiary of Carolyn Micklem Scholarship, and her works have appeared or forthcoming in *Strange Horizons, FIYAH, Uncanny Magazine, Poetry Daily, Agbowo, Poetry Wales, Torch Literary Arts, Utopia Science Fiction Magazine, Arc Poetry Magazine*, and elsewhere. This is her second chapbook. She is active on X @ZainabBobi and Instagram @zaynab_iliyasu_bobi